Amaryllis of Hawaii Loves to Cook
"Recipes for Life"
By Marilyn Jansen

Amaryllis of Hawaii loves to cook and prepare parties and entertain for others. It can be dinner for two or a party for fifty. She can handle. Her adventures in the kitchen began at about age twelve. She was asked to peel an onion once at a friend's house. She didn't know how, but she learned fast.

Over the years she has been very receptive to learning about the culinary arts. She loves the joy of cooking and the beautiful presentation of food. Amaryllis enjoys reading cookbooks & browsing through magazines for recipes & ideas. She saves them in her dream books of future possibilities. It's so important to visualize and believe in the possibilities. If you can imagine and believe something possible, you can achieve it. So dream it up, whatever you wish, and find images or recipes to make it happen. Look at them often to surround yourself with stimulating ideas and beauty in your subconscious mind. When people tell Amaryllis they don't know how to cook, she thinks, my God, all you have to know is the basics of cooking to make wonderful meals creatively and easily. What we eat defines so much about us. Our culture and lifestyle are expressed by the way we prepare our food. People are so busy taking care of business that many seem to lose the joy of cooking, opting for fast foods, when homemade is so much better. There are so many ways to learn, we can all become chefs at home.

We have the Food Network, Hawaii Cooks, and we are continuously introduced to delicious food preparations on television, in books, magazines, and other people's homes. Families pass on recipes from generation to generation, and friends learn from each other.

It's all about the home, and we love it.

We realize that family is most important, and living for today is essential to a satisfying life. For an artist, everything is approached creatively, and this brings such joy and happiness to Amaryllis. She will show you, with an artistic approach, how anyone can be a wonderful cook and can prepare parties and entertain with ease.

CHICKEN SOUP

1 large whole chicken
5 stalks celery
1 large onion quartered
4 large carrots
4 cloves garlic crushed
fresh thyme, sage, dill, tarragon, cilantro,
salt & pepper
4 medium potatoes
1 yam 1 parsnip 1 rutubaga
green onions
lemons

garnish with fresh cilantro, green onions or parsley!

Chicken Soup

Once upon a time, long, long ago, Amaryllis had a friend who taught her how to make a good soup from scratch. It happened one day when she was feeling down. Her friend came to her and said, "Amaryllis, what you need is a nice chicken soup." They shopped for fresh vegetables, like celery, onions, carrots, garlic, potatoes, parsnips, rutabagas, and a whole chicken. At home, they started by crushing the garlic, quartering the onions, and put big pieces of celery with the leaves, and whole carrots, all together into a big pot with the whole, cleaned chicken and covered these with water. The three main ingredients for just about any soup are celery, onions, and carrots. (It's a Trio). Bring it to a boil, skim off any impurities (the foam on top), turn it down, add fresh thyme and simmer for about an hour. She removes the bones to the side, discards the discolored celery, and tastes the broth to see how it's coming along. Then she adds salt and pepper, and new chopped celery and carrots to re-season. Amaryllis also adds the potatoes and other vegetables at this time. Mmmmm; it always develops such a nice flavor. It is important not to cook it too long. One and 1/2 hours maximum, at a simmer, will keep the flavor bright. She squeezes a lemon to brighten the soup, adds fresh cilantro, dill weed, or fresh parsley. Be spontaneous! Sometimes she adds noodles or stars or bows for the last ten minutes, or cooked rice at the end.

Cooking a wonderful soup for a friend will cheer them up, and nourish the *body, mind, soul and spirit* for both of you.

This chicken soup is made into Mexican tortilla soup by adding a trio of tomatoes, jalapenos, and onions, which she has sautéed, at the 1-hour cooking time. When serving into bowls, she tops with avocado, fresh squeezed lime juice, cilantro, and corn tortilla strips that have been fried in oil and drained. Delicious!

Amaryllis makes her Thai hot chile lemongrass soup from the basic chicken soup. Thai chile paste is made from:

12 chopped green jalapeno chiles
2 tbsp oil
fresh chopped ginger
5 kaffir lime leaves
1/2 tsp kaffir lime zest
4 stalks chopped lemon grass
2 cloves garlic
3 shallots, sliced
1/2 tsp ground coriander
1/2 tsp caraway seeds
1 tbsp sugar
2 tbsp fish sauce

Blend in a food processor. This paste can be stored for two weeks. Thai chile paste can be bought in Asian sections of the grocery store, in green or red chili versions. She starts with 2 tbsp. chili paste in 2 tbsp. hot oil, sautes cubed tofu or shrimp for a couple of minutes in the oil, and then adds the liquids (*4 cups chicken broth*, 2 tbsp. more fish sauce, water, and 1 can *coconut milk*). She heats for 10 minutes and serves with a garnish of Thai basil, cilantro or mint.

Always add the fresh greens to the chicken soup in the last 5 minutes, so the color is bright!

Taste it at one hour.

Re-season with freshly chopped celery, salt & pepper a squeeze of lemon, and fresh herbs & spices.

Take out the bones and discolored vegetables.

Always keep lemons in the house!

Grow your own fresh herbs!

Very Veggie Soup

Amaryllis makes a vegetable soup from water, carrots, celery, onions, garlic, tomatoes (crushed, fresh or canned), and tomato sauce, yams or sweet potatoes. Sometimes whatever is in the refrigerator determines the soup! She adds ketchup & vinegar and a little sugar to enrich the flavor! Fresh herbs and spices always enhance her cooking! Basil is wonderful with tomatoes. The freshness of garden veggies, fresh herbs and garlic is delightful. There's nothing like good home-made soup to warm everyone and fill them with great nutrition. Saute garlic, onions and celery in 2 tbsp. oil, add all the ingredients and simmer 1 hour. Remove bay leaf and add more chopped celery, taste and season with salt, pepper and spices, garnish with fresh greens! Top with cheese, croutons, or crackers!

two tbsp vegetable oil
6 cloves garlic, minced
1 large onion, slivered
5 medium carrots, chopped
3 ribs celery, chopped
1 sweet potato or yam, chopped
8 cups water
16 oz. tomato sauce
16 oz. whole tomatoes
1/4 c. ketchup, 1/4 c. vinegar and 2 tbsp. sugar
1 bay leaf, peppercorns, garlic-parsley powder
tarragon, chives, dill, basil, or curry
Try eggplant & mushrooms!

Be Inventive! Make it your own!

Puree seasoned vegetables and add cream to make rich soups!

The Basics

Amaryllis would teach anyone that the secret to a healthy diet is a balance of protein, fresh vegetables and fruits, whole grains, low fat intake, and lots of pure water daily to cleanse the body.

She doesn't advocate strict vegetarianism, but does encourage a majority of veggies in the diet, with very little meat as a protein source. She loves soybeans.

She would teach everyone that there are so many ways to get adequate protein without meat. She learned that, in many countries, protein is derived from plant sources.

She learned that, by combining many sources of protein throughout the day, vegetarians could obtain plenty of protein. Certain foods combined double the protein content.

In Mexico, Rice and beans and corn tortillas created a complete protein.

She learned that by adding 1/4 cup whole wheat berries to 3/4 cup brown rice, she could double the protein.

Nuts are an excellent source of protein. Sesame seeds add protein. Wheat germ added to cereal increases the protein and fiber.

Eggs are the most complete protein.

Three-Cheese Yellow Squash Dish

This is a wonderful, colorful, yellow crookneck squash casserole made with eggs, cottage cheese, monterey jack cheese, and Parmesan cheese.

She slices fresh, young, firm yellow crookneck squashes 1/4 inch thick and lines a 9x9 baking pan with them. She whisks 6 eggs and mixes 8 oz. cottage cheese into the eggs, with salt & pepper. She pours 1/3 of the mixture over the first layer of squash, then sprinkles a layer of jack cheese over it. She layers more yellow crookneck squash, with slices of onion, and pours over another 1/3 of the cottage cheese-egg mixture and tops it with jack cheese and Parmesan. Finally, she adds the last layer and tops with jack cheese, Parmesan and bread crumbs, then bakes at 375 degrees for 45 minutes, until all the cheeses are melted and the eggs are cooked. This is a wonderful vegetable entree or side dish!

6 eggs
8 oz. cottage cheese
8 oz. Jack cheese
1/2 cup Parmesan cheese
6 yellow crookneck squash
1 yellow onion sliced
bread crumbs
salt & pepper

Mix the eggs with the cottage cheese
Layer the sliced squash and pour it over them.
Add grated Jack cheese over each layer
and top with Parmesan & breadcrumbs
Bake at 375 degrees for 45 minutes
or until eggs are done.

Some of us still love the great flavors of a little meat and fish, of course, so we enjoy them. In Hawaii, the fish is so awesome, we have many ways to enjoy it! We broil fish, grill it, or eat raw sashimi as an appetizer. We can sauté or make a sauce to pour over it. We bake it in the oven wrapped in foil, or in ti-leaves on the grill.

Hawaii is such an exciting place to live because of all the ethnicities. It is a Pacific Islander place, with people from all over the world. It is a culture of the outdoors. The beauty is so great and the temperature is perfect!

Trade winds blow the air so clean. The ocean is full of fresh fish. Fresh fruits abound. Citrus and mango, coconut, pineapple, lilikoi (passion fruit), guava and bananas are plentiful.

We cook and season simple delicious foods from the sea, accompanied by fresh grilled fruits, and a bowl of poi. Seaweed is used for seasoning in Poke, a mixture of raw fish chunks, sesame seeds, sesame oil, macadamia nuts, kukui nuts, soy sauce, green onions, and limu (seaweed) gives it the saltiness of the sea.

Sometimes Amaryllis prepares fresh ahi (yellow fin tuna).

On the Big Island of Hawaii, the waters are very deep off shore. Ahi is prevalent. It is delivered to the markets so fresh. She can tell it is fresh by its beautiful red color, its firmness, and the fresh smell of the sea.

At home, she prepares part of her filets as a *sashimi platter.*

She slices it very thin and arranges it in a circle around the edge of a plate. She mixes soy sauce and wasabi in a small rice bowl in the center, placed on a bed of shredded cabbage or shredded daikon radish.

She serves this with boiled soybeans.

Grilled Ahi

Season ahi steaks with minced garlic, salt and pepper, and dried dill, basil or thyme. Brush or drizzle with extra virgin olive oil. Sear in the flavor of the delicious fish on the grill or in a grill pan on medium-high heat.

Add a few splashes of Chardonnay to poach the fish. Fish should never be overcooked, but just to perfection.

After searing the fish on a high heat, Amaryllis transfers it, with all its juices, to the oven in a baking dish to cook for 10 minutes at 375 degrees, or just covers the pan and continues cooking for 10 minutes. She adds a sprig of cilantro for the last minute or two.

She *serves with white steamed rice and a fresh green vegetable* or salad, with her homemade vinaigrette of course.

Fish is grilled, baked, poached, sautéed, or even fried.
Some prefer it raw inside as seared ahi, rolled in many different
things, like sesame, seaweed (nori), or salmon roe.

Amaryllis likes Ono cooked to perfection, seared on the
outside, or a macadamia-nut, panko-crust preparation.

At Uncle Billie's Polynesian Restaurant in Hilo, she
had the most delicious mahi mahi with a macadamia-nut
béchamel.
She has tasted fresh fish at many restaurants in the islands
throughout Hawaii.

At Mama's Fish House, on Maui her favorite is the Hawaiian-
style preparation of the mahi-mahi soaked in coconut milk and
wrapped with luau (taro leaf) and steamed inside the ti-leaf.
Mmmmm, it is so delicious and moist.

Served with grilled pineapple, grilled apple banana, a slice of
dark purple sweet potato, and a coconut shell-bowl of poi to
complete the beautiful presentation, it is simply elegant.

She is excited she lives on one of the most beautiful islands in the
world, and there is such creativity coming out of Hawaii, it is hard
not to have it rub off on you.

She loves the creativity at Cafe O'Lei.
Haliimaile General Store has a touch of old Maui.
Kula Lodge has magnificent views! Wailea has the best sunsets!
From Napili you see beautiful Molokai.

Chefs abound.

Hotel Hana Maui is casual elegance! Lahaina and Kaanapali have fun places everywhere.

We have the local-style ethnic foods of Hawaii, Portugal, the Philippines, Japan, China, California, Mexico, South America, France and being on the Rim of the Pacific, we combine a little bit of it all.

We have many vegetarian influences to inspire us with aromatic recipes and whole grain dishes from India, South East Asia and other countries around the world.

Mango-Pineapple Salsa

1 large mango cubed
4 oz. small pineapple chunks
jalapeno chili, minced
2 fresh basil leaves, minced
2 tsp. fresh lime juice
pepper
2 tsp. sugar
2 tsp. vinegar
fresh cilantro

Mix together and chill to let the flavors blend for a few hours with fresh cilantro. This is excellent served over fish or chicken!

Mahi-Mahi, Coconut Style

in Ti-Leaf Package

Mahi is a beautiful, white, flaky fish caught fresh from the waters of the clean ocean surrounding the Hawaiian Islands. In Mexico, it is called Dorado. It is a colorful blue and yellow fish when fresh from the sea. We prepare it many ways, but this is a favorite Polynesian style.

4 eight oz. mahi-mahi filets
8 large ti leaves with rib removed
lemon grass, chopped
ginger, chopped
garlic, minced
lime juice
cilantro
sesame oil
coconut milk

Lay the mahi on a ti leaf, with lemon grass, ginger, garlic, cilantro and lime juice. Pour coconut milk over filet and a few drops sesame oil.
Tie ti-leaf and wrap with another ti-leaf using rib to tie; then steam or grill for 10-15 minutes.

Serve with steamed white jasmine or calrose rice and mango salsa!

Whole Fish
Steamed Opakapaka

It is not difficult to prepare a whole fish. This is how we can serve many people with ease. Amaryllis learned to prepare dinner for twelve her first time in the Bay Area, when she served whole, baked salmon caught fresh from the sea. This was so easy to prepare! The cleaned fish (gutted, with head removed) was stuffed with whole mushrooms, slices of onions, dried sweet basil, and pieces of butter. The fish was dotted with butter and basil, then covered in foil to bake for 30 minutes at 375 degrees! She would look in to see that the fish was pink and moist and perfectly cooked. The sweet basil was so fragrant! To serve, she would cut into 2-inch sections for each person. The mushrooms and onions and buttery juices were drizzled on top of each serving and garnished with lemon wedges. She served a green salad and wild rice.

In Hawaii, she discovered the moist, deep water fish opakapaka, or Hawaiian pink snapper. Hawaii's seafood has been described as the best in the world! The islands are so remote and the waters so clean. The fish are awesome. She loves steamed opakapaka with a black bean sauce. Black- bean sauce is easy to prepare. She uses 4 tbsp. salted, dried, black beans and 2 and 1/2 cups of water. Boil these in a frying pan, add 1 tbsp. cornstarch to thicken, then add chopped green onions. One tsp. of sugar is added. Cook 5 minutes. The whole cleaned, scaled fish is rubbed with Hawaiian salt and steamed in a long fish-steamer for 20 minutes. The fish is scored, salted black bean sauce and green onions are poured over it, then drizzled with hot peanut oil and served on a platter. Guests can pick at the fish with chopsticks!

Banana Pancakes

Anyone can make beautiful banana pancakes.
Use fresh flour and baking powder. Sift dry ingredients.

1 & 1/2 cups flour	1 cup milk
3 tbsp. sugar	1 tsp. vanilla
2 tsp. baking powder	2 bananas, sliced
1 tsp. salt	2 eggs

Mix wet into dry ingredients just until blended. Add bananas and ladle onto a hot oiled griddle or pan. You know it's hot enough when a drop of water bounces off the pan.
Let bubbles appear on the pancakes before you flip them. Drizzle with syrup and dust with powdered sugar.

Try blueberries, apples, peaches, or mango in pancakes or wrapped in crepes!

Basic crepe batter

2 eggs	1/2 cup flour
2/3 cup milk	1/4 tsp. salt
1 tbsp. oil	

Lightly beat the eggs, stir in milk & oil, gradually stir in flour and salt. Beat until smooth. Cover and refrigerate 2 hours. Brush a 7-inch crepe pan with oil and heat until hot. Stir batter, add scant 2 tbsp. batter to pan & quickly tilt to cover bottom of pan. Cook crepe, turning over until lightly browned on both sides. Makes 12

A loha

L iving in Hawaii is a gift that must be shared!

O ne way is to express ourselves creatively!

H awaii is a hot spot in the universe for cuisine.

A maryllis loves to learn everything she can about the foods of Hawaii. Reviewing restaurants and Pacific Rim Cuisine helps add to her own style.

Basil Mayo-Salmon Filets

for two persons:

2 salmon filets
olive oil
salt & pepper
garlic flakes
balsamic vinegar
mayonnaise
fresh basil or dried herbs
italian bread crumbs

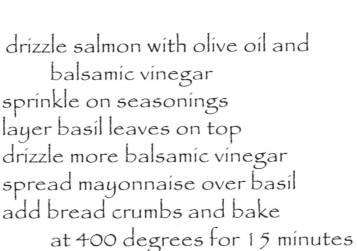

drizzle salmon with olive oil and
    balsamic vinegar
sprinkle on seasonings
layer basil leaves on top
drizzle more balsamic vinegar
spread mayonnaise over basil
add bread crumbs and bake
    at 400 degrees for 15 minutes

She places the filets in a baking pan.

She sprinkles with garlic flakes, salt and pepper, fresh or dried basil or other herbs like tarragon, dill, or curry. (She grows sweet basil and uses it often).

She prefers fresh leaves of sweet basil, sprinkled with a little garlic powder, drizzled with extra virgin olive oil and balsamic vinegar, and a tbsp. of mayonnaise spread over the basil to keep it moist.

Top with breadcrumbs (Italian kind) and bake at 400 degrees for 15 minutes, exactly. It is delicious!

Immediately served on a bed of steamed white rice, with buttered asparagus or broccoli and fresh squeezed lemon, or a fresh salad of mesclun greens or Bibb lettuce with honey vinaigrette, is wonderful! A glass of Chardonnay goes perfectly.

Iced tea with a sprig of mint or a slice of lemon is refreshing!

It's the extra attention to details that matters.

(Cut into 2 inch squares, for appetizers!)

Every complete meal has protein, like meat, fish or tofu prepared as a main dish, with carbohydrates as side dishes. Whole grains and leafy green vegetables are the Good Carbs. They require energy to digest and therefore do not turn to sugar quickly as other, highly processed foods, like white flour products that have the bran removed from the wheat grain. Remember: whole grains are best! We can still enjoy our favorites like white rice in small quantities and an occasional pastry or delicious pancake.

Vegetarians make a main dish of vegetables, legumes, pastas and grains with proteins like cheese, nuts, or tofu.

One must know how to plan and prepare a basic meal, in order to know how to cook.

Amaryllis likes lots of color and freshness in her kitchen.

There are always fresh fruits in bowls, and fresh vegetables in her refrigerator or straight from the garden.

She can prepare beautiful meals daily because she keeps her pantry stocked with spices, extra virgin olive oil, a variety of vinegars, and has a fresh herb garden nearby and a salad garden too. She always keeps garlic, lemons and honey. She stores yams and potatoes in the produce drawer, with carrots, celery, onions, turnips at times, radishes and daikon, and shops frequently for fresh vegetables at open markets in Hawaii.
We have Japanese eggplant, watercress, and green beans in many varieties. Chinese greens are abundant. Napa cabbage is a favorite. Snap peas, snow peas, corn in season, Okinawan purple potatoes, dried beans, squashes and many unusual fruits like cherimoya, star fruit, and even jack fruit are found. She loves the Maui swap meet to find interesting local vegetables and gets to meet the people who grow them. On Maui, there are open markets in Wailuku, Kihei, Kahului, Napili and the scheduling varies. Sometimes she buys at Pukalani Superette, Long's or K-Mart, and there is always Costco.
Foodland has a nice selection. There's Down to Earth, Mana Foods and Hawaiian Moons for organic produce. She loves to buys grains in bulk, and herb teas, and exotic items.

She stops at signs saying fresh corn or broccoli for sale! Find the open markets near you!

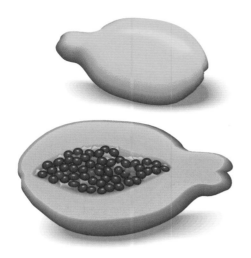

Grow your own!

She prefers her fruits and vegetables organically grown
(without pesticides or heavy chemical fertilizers).

So growing her own is the best!

She grows lettuces, Chinese greens, a mesclun mix, and green onions, chives, basil, Roma tomatoes, Kabocha pumpkins, daikon, turnips, sunflowers, zinnias, cosmos, carrots, peppers (all kinds), papayas, mints, sage, thyme, and lavender, snow peas, snap peas, zucchini & crookneck squash.

Once you know how to prepare basic fish, chicken, and meat dishes, with fresh herbs and spices, and use basic ingredients like olive oil, vinegar, fresh lemons and limes, and serve with rice, potatoes, or pastas, and fresh vegetables of all kinds, steamed, sautéed, blanched, roasted or baked, you'll be on your way to being a gourmet cook!

Miso Dip

In Hawaii, there are always many varieties of fresh green beans. They are wonderful blanched for 2 minutes, plunged into ice water, drained, then served with miso dip made with miso paste, rice vinegar, sugar, sesame oil, and water.

2 tbsp. light miso paste
2 tbsp. sugar
2 tbsp. rice wine vinegar
4 tbsp. water
Mix & taste. Add sesame oil, sugar and water as needed.

Buttermilk dressing

Make your own ranch dressing! It is awesome with fresh tomatoes and greens from the garden.

1 cup buttermilk   minced green onion   salt & pepper
1 cup mayonnaise   1 tsp. garlic powder   fresh parsely
2 cloves garlic   1/4 tsp. cayenne

Mince garlic, chop parsley and combine all.
Whisk to blend, chill and serve over veggies.

Dill Dip

1 pint sour cream   2 tbsp. sugar
1/2 cup mayonnaise   2 tbsp. dill weed
2 tsp powdered ginger
fresh lemon, squeezed   "Dill, dill, dill lots of dill!"

Dill dip is excellent with fresh vegetable platters.

Fresh Fresh Fresh

To have a healthy body, mind, soul, and spirit, one must eat plenty of beautiful fresh fruits and vegetables.

Choose those with shiny skin, young and tender, bright in color, and looking full of life.

Immediately after eating fresh lettuce or spinach greens, Amaryllis feels so excellent.

A salad of fresh greens with home-grown tomatoes, fresh basil, fresh garlic, a little feta cheese, raisins, sliced celery, green onions, thinly sliced carrot coins, or julienned zucchini, cucumbers or roasted red and yellow peppers, and her awesome honey vinaigrette is a meal in itself.

She uses varieties of greens like spinach, arugula, Bibb lettuce, romaine and mesclun mixes. Learn to wash these lettuces gently by rinsing in a bath of cool water then drying in the colander placed above a bowl to drain.

Amaryllis sets her greens in front of the kitchen window so the trade winds can blow them dry, or gently pats them with paper towels to dry.

It is important not to crush your greens, or squeeze them.

Handle these beauties with the care they deserve.

Green Layered Salad

(all greens washed & dried)

1 head Romaine lettuce   1 head Bibb lettuce
1 head bronz-leaf lettuce
1 Mesclun mix (arugula, tatsoi, mizuna, chervil)
fresh spinach leaves
fresh basil leaves, Italian flat-leaf parsley, dill weed
Cucumbers, sliced thin
Bermuda (red) onion, sliced thin, or Maui sweet onion
Zucchini, carrots, roasted peppers, sliced or julienned
Feta cheese, crumbled
Raisins
Vine-ripened tomatoes
3 garlic cloves crushed
Extra virgin olive oil
Balsamic Vinegar
Fresh squeezed lemon juice

(For two persons, just use a few leaves of each lettuce!)
 Layer greens on a platter with roughly chopped fresh herbs
and crushed garlic, drizzle with olive oil, balsamic vinegar, and
lemon juice. Layer with other ingredients and repeat.
Add salt and fresh pepper. Crumble feta and top with raisins.
Drizzle honey vinaigrette! Add Mandarin oranges!

Honey Vinaigrette

For 2 persons:

- 1/4 cup extra virgin olive oil
- Balsamic vinegar (4-5 tablespoons)
- 1-2 whole fresh-squeezed lemons
- 1 clove fresh garlic, crushed or minced.
- 2 tbsp. honey and a little salt and pepper.
- Fresh or dried herbs (dill, tarragon, or basil).
- Whisk together and pour on just before serving!

Double this for big salads!
She mixes this dressing almost daily for her salads.

Remember, fresh is best! Amaryllis learned long ago, from friends in the San Francisco Bay Area, that a freshly prepared dressing was something very special and easily made.

Basically, all that is needed is a good oil, vinegar, lemons, limes, or any citrus juices, salt and pepper, fresh or dried herbs, and sometimes the addition of sugar or honey, and a clove of garlic, crushed. Then whisk it all together briskly to emulsify the mixture and give your wonderful greens even more delicious flavor and brightness. Try guava or lilikoi juice!

Broccoli with fresh squeezed lemon and Parmesan

1 head fresh green broccoli florets
melted butter
1 lemon
Parmesan cheese
mayonnaise
pinch of sugar

Prepare the broccoli in salted boiling water with a pinch of sugar for about 4 minutes, or until a fork can just pierce the stem and the color is bright green. Immediately plunge into ice water to stop the cooking or serve immediately with fresh squeezed lemon, drizzled butter and Parmesan with a dollop of mayo on the side! She learned this from a New York chef. She loves to serve it with baked herb-roasted chicken breasts and yams, too. The colors are incredible.

Cole Slaw

1 large cabbage, shredded & chopped
2 tbsp. sugar
1 tbsp. white vinegar
5 tbsp. mayonnaise
Mix together in a large bowl, taste and add sugar or vinegar, if needed. Chill for an hour before serving.
Her mom taught her this one. It's cool and refreshing with any meal!

Veggies

Steam, bake, grill or broil your veggies to keep their flavor. Brush thin sliced eggplant with olive oil; grill, then roll around a stuffing of mozzarella cheese, roasted red peppers, Roma tomatoes, Parmesan, and breadcrumbs drizzled with more olive oil. Heat in the oven or covered grill.

Amaryllis learned, from a chef at a Malibu wedding, about roasting red and yellow peppers. She observed him rolling those peppers on the open flame on the gas stove and thought wow, that is neat!

She loved the smell and the sight of the blackened skin. It was dramatic and tasted so flavorful. These are added to salads or Italian sandwiches drizzled with red wine vinegar and extra virgin olive oil. Delicious!

She knew that steaming retains the nutrients in veggies. She knew that microwaving vegetables can do that also. She knew that vegetables tasted best when hardly cooked!

She loves bright green broccoli. She trims the flowerets off the trunk, steams them in salted boiling water for a couple of minutes, and serves immediately or plunges them into cold water to stop the cooking process, and quickly reheats them at serving time. She learned that a pinch of sugar enhances the flavor and the salted water enhances the color. It gets rinsed off anyway.

Amaryllis squeezes lemon over these green jewels to keep the color and flavor, drizzles them with hot melted butter, sprinkles on Parmesan, and serves with a small dollop of mayo on the side. It has crisp, wonderful texture and bright flavor.

Presentation is Everything!

Food must be served beautifully. It appears appetizing when it is fresh, colorful, the right temperature, in the right portions and combinations of textures and flavors that compliment one another.

Fresh flowers on the table make a room look beautiful.

A lovely table has a tablecloth and/or nice place mats, clean silverware, glasses, and stemware when serving wine. Beautiful eclectic collections of glassware are wonderful for creating atmosphere.

Hawaiians create a beautiful table by arranging large ti leaves as a covering on the table to present platters of seafood, Kahlua pork, and lomi-lomi salmon among scattered flowers of plumeria, ginger, orchids, and fresh fruits like pineapples, bananas, and breadfruit.

An artistic setting can be created almost anywhere.

At home, or by the sea, a cabin in the mountains, or in an apartment at a university, beauty is achieved with a few nice touches.

Learning from Friends

Amaryllis has learned from many people over the years, and certain recipes have stayed with her for life.

This is how you create your own style.

Learn from others and adapt to your own lifestyle.

She learned to make an awesome marinara sauce for spaghetti many years ago. It was different from the sauce her dad had made with ground beef or Italian sausages. She liked the bright tomatoes and herb flavors and the heartiness of mushrooms and thick sauce without meat.

Create a bruscetta with sliced tomatoes, red onion, and fresh basil. Drizzle extra virgin olive oil on these and toss together. Brush French bread with extra virgin olive oil and toast both sides. Serve on toasted slices of French bread. It's a salad on toast!

Marinara Ingredients

6-8 cloves garlic
a large yellow onion, slivered

2 tbsp. vegetable or olive oil

tomato sauce, 16 oz.
(sometimes tomato paste 1 can)

crushed or stewed tomatoes or
whole tomatoes 1-2 cans
(or fresh Roma tomatoes blanched)

20 fresh, large Mushrooms

Fresh or dried rosemary, oregano,
sweet basil, and a bay leaf or mixed
Italian spices. (Fresh basil is best!)

Parmesan for topping!

Garlic Bread is made by melting butter in a
pan with slivers of fresh garlic, then pouring this over 2 long
French breads and broiling on low until golden brown!

Parmesan can be added for more flavor!

Marinara

She starts by mincing several (6-8) cloves of garlic , cutting onions into quarters, and then slicing these quarters into slivers.

She heats up her large frying pan or electric skillet, adds olive oil and the garlic while it is cold, so the garlic doesn't burn.

She adds the slivered onions and cooks them until they are translucent, then adds thickly sliced, thoroughly cleaned mushrooms.

Marinara means without meat. The mushrooms give the sauce a lot of body. She adds two 8 oz. cans of tomato sauce and a can of stewed, crushed tomatoes, or whole tomatos. Sometimes she adds homegrown Roma tomatoes that she had blanched to remove the skin and saved in Ziploc bags in the freezer. Roma tomatoes make wonderful sauces. If the sauce needs thickening she uses a can of tomato paste.

She simmers these ingredients for about 15 minutes, then adds her Italian herbs and spices. (Oregano, rosemary, thyme, basil, and a bay leaf.) She crushes these in her hand to release the essence of the flavor.
Later she adds fresh torn basil leaves into the rich red sauce and drizzles more olive oil over all.

She simmers for at least an hour on low.

Soon the aromas are filling the house, and all the senses are stimulated.

She loves to cook Italian cuisine, crushing garlic, and feeling so earthy using fresh herbs and spices.

She continues the evening with an Italian film in the theatre. Films influenced her!

She loves foreign films that show all the cooking. It is so enriching to read about other cultures and see how they live.

Some travel the entire world, and others travel in their imaginations through films and books and art that enrich their lives with beauty and culture.

Pasta

There are so many types of pastas. Spaghetti takes about 10 minutes to cook. Angel hair pasta, much thinner, takes about 2 minutes. Fresh pastas cook fast. Some macaronis, fettuccine, linguini, ravioli, penne, bows and shells, have spinach and vegetables added to the flour to give color and flavor. Start with a large pot of salted water, and a few tablespoons of olive oil to prevent the pasta from sticking together. The most important thing to learn about pasta is to cook it "al dente". This is when the teeth can just bite through it, not overcooked and soft. She tests a strand of spaghetti by removing it, cooling slightly, and taking a bite. She drains the pasta into a colander, and quickly returns it to the pot with the heat turned off, leaving a small amount of water in the pot to avoid drying out. She serves each person a generous portion, and ladles the sauce over each. Freshly grated Parmesan cheese is delicious. Garlic bread or fresh Italian rolls are wonderful to dip in the sauce.

She found pasta didn't always need an elaborate sauce to go over it. She prepares sauce with olive oil, fresh garlic, lemon juice, and capers. A pesto sauce made from basil leaves, olive oil, pine nuts, garlic and parmesan blended in a food processor was so fragrant and green! Lemon juice kept the color beautiful!

She prepares Pasta Primavera, which means Spring in the Latin languages, by roasting all kinds of fresh red, yellow and green peppers in the oven on a baking sheet, with Roma tomatoes, onions, and fresh herbs drizzled with olive oil and minced garlic and sprinkled with grated Romano or Parmesan, for about a half-hour, then tosses them all together on a bed of pasta. It is so fragrant and the colors filled her kitchen with beauty!

How to make a Caesar Salad

Prepare croutons by cutting 6 slices of bread into cubes, coating with olive oil, fresh and dried herbs & minced garlic and bake at 350 degrees for about 20 minutes, turning often.

- 1 large head Romaine
- 10-12 cloves of garlic (some for croutons)
- Worcestershire sauce (a few shakes)
- Parmesan, fresh grated 3/4 cup
  & 1/3 cup, powdered
- 6 slices of bread for croutons
- fresh or dried herbs for croutons
- 2 lemons and 1 small egg added just before tossing
- 2-3 tbsp. olive oil or vegetable oil for salad and croutons.

Combine washed, dried and chilled Romaine with garlic cloves, Worcestershire, lemon juice, Parmesan, and oil. Toss. Then add the lightly beaten egg to bind all the ingredients. Taste and add more lemon juice as needed.
She has used anchovy paste for a salty flavor!

It is never soggy if enough lettuce is used.
Just before serving, she adds crisp herbed croutons to everyone's delight. We love this salad.
It takes a little effort, but is better than any other Caesar she has ever tasted.

She serves Pasta Marinara with a green salad, like a Caesar salad; and a hearty red wine such as a Cabernet Sauvignon, or Merlot, or a fragrant, young, red Gamay Beaujolais, or Zinfandel, with a lot of sediment.

Caesar Salad

Amaryllis learned from her friend Marcia how to make the awesome Caesar Salad. Start with a very large head of Romaine. Remove the leaves, rinse them and set them in a colander to dry, or use a salad spinner, and chill them. Then Amaryllis prepares her croutons by cutting six slices of fresh bread into cubes. She uses wheat or white, whatever she has on hand. She places them on a baking sheet and sprinkles on lots of minced garlic, and a spice called beau monde, or thyme, basil, dill weed, oregano, rosemary, garlic powder, salt and pepper, drizzles with olive or vegetable oil, and tosses them to coat the bread so it will toast nicely in the oven, at 350 degrees for 20-30 minutes. She turns them often so they don't burn, and makes sure the herbs get distributed evenly. While the croutons are in the oven, she crushes more garlic for the salad. She tears the Romaine for the salad into a wooden salad bowl, adds the garlic, a few shakes of Worcestershire sauce, two tbsp. oil and squeezes on fresh lemon juice, careful not to let any seeds fall in, then adds the fresh grated Parmesan and the lightly beaten egg. She re-seasons with salt and pepper and adds the croutons. Awesome Salad!

Pineapple Carrot Cake

2 cups flour
2 tsp. baking powder
1-1/2 tsp. baking soda
1 tsp. salt
2 tsp. cinnamon
1-1/2 cups sugar

1- 1/2 cups oil
4 eggs, beaten
1 cup crushed pineapple
2 cups grated carrot
1 cup chopped nuts & raisins
1/2 cup honey

Sift together dry ingredients. Add oil and eggs and mix well.
Stir in pineapple, carrots, nuts and raisins.
Pour into greased and floured 9 x 13 inch pan or bundt pan.
Bake at 350 degrees for 40 minutes, until toothpick comes
out clean.

Cool and frost with cream cheese frosting.

Cream Cheese Frosting:
1/2 cup butter (1 stick)
1 8 oz. pkg. cream cheese

1 tsp. vanilla
1 box powdered sugar

Beat until fluffy and frost the cake.

The Pineapple is the symbol of hospitality!

Hawaiian Style

In Hawaii, her eyes were opened to an entire new world that inspired and awakened all her senses.

At 18 years old, she learned to use chopsticks. She tried saimin. She learned that the Japanese pickled turnips, ginger, and many vegetables.

She tried her first ahi sashimi and loved it. Yellowfin Tuna is her favorite raw fish. It's da best! The Japanese must have it! In winter the seas are rough and the price of Ahi goes up. No matter, they still gotta have it!

In Hawaii there is Hawaiian food and what we call local-style plate lunches. At a traditional Hawaiian luau, there will always be a big pig cooked in an imu (underground oven).
The pig is wrapped in moist banana leaves and chicken wire and covered with smooth rocks. To cook, the pig is placed into the hot coals of a fire built before hand.

Lomi-lomi salmon is prepared, along with sweet potatoes (purple, white and yellow). There's lau lau, a Ti-leaf package containing fish, chicken or pork wrapped with taro leaves.

She loves lau lau. The flavor of the taro leaf is so ono. (delicious!).

Kahlua pork (pig) has such a delicious smoky flavor, and it is so moist from being wrapped in the wet leaves underground.

Hawaiians are the essence of graciousness.

Among Hawaiians, everyone shares.

That is the Hawaiian Style.
It has been passed on for generations.

When Amaryllis arrived here, she learned about it right away.

Because of this graciousness anyone feels welcome here.

Though she experienced culture shock upon arrival, after
seeing the prices in the grocery stores, she learned quickly how
to get along and that she would get by with her ingenuity and
by learning from the people who lived here.

If somebody has mangos, they share. If someone has green
onions growing, they share. Local people are just like that.

Sometimes her boyfriend's family would drop by
bananas. Another day she would find a bag of green
beans hanging on the door, or
green onions wrapped in newspaper
from Mr. Kanemoto.

It's so nice.

Though it isn't like it used to be
in Hawaii,
some things, like sharing,
go on an on.

Namasu

2 cucumbers, sliced thin
1 sweet yellow onion, sliced thin
1 carrot, sliced thin or julienned (optional)
    (or radishes, sliced celery, and tomatoes)
1/3 cup white vinegar or rice wine vinegar
1/2 cup water
2 tbsp. sugar

Combine all and chill before serving
with lomi-lomi salmon, poi, and sliced tofu with a
soy wasabe dipping sauce.

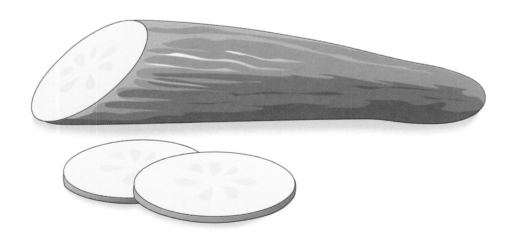

The blending of this culture started back in the old days when the sugar cane field workers would sit down to lunch in the fields. Every person of a different culture would put some of their food into the middle for everyone to share. It was learned from the loving nature of the Native Hawaiians who took more joy in giving than in receiving!

So today we have a special blend of foods that are unique to Hawaii that we all love and enjoy!

Hawaiian Style now includes Portuguese Bean Soup, Maki Sushi, Spam Musubi, Kim Chee, Sashimi, Potato-Mac Salad, Kahlua Pork, Lomi-lomi Salmon, Poi, Chow-Fun, Saimin, Manapua, Lau lau, Poke, Miso, Papio, Teriyaki, Ono, Ahi, Mahi-Mahi, Onaga, Opah, Ulua, Opakapaka & Namasu.

She read and listened to the oral histories often.

She experienced how loving Hawaiians are.

Somen Salad

One package Somen Noodles
One head Bibb lettuce or Romaine
1 cucumber
2 green onions

(Drop noodles into boiling water for 2-4 minutes)
Drain immediately and rinse under cool water.
Set in colander to drain thoroughly.
Prepare a bed of clean dried lettuce leaves.
Add Somen noodles on top.
Add sliced cucumber & green onions.
Pour Oriental dressing over all, and toss!

Oriental Dressing
1/4 cup sesame oil
4 tbsp. vegetable oil
1/4 cup soy sauce
1/4 cup rice wine vinegar
1/4 cup sugar or substitute
1 tbsp. light miso paste (optional)
Whisk vigorously to blend !

Oriental Salad
1 head napa cabbage
1/4 head red cabbage
1 bunch green onions
1 bunch cilantro

Shred the cabbages. Slice the onions lengthwise and chop with cilantro.

Mix together and pour on dressing.

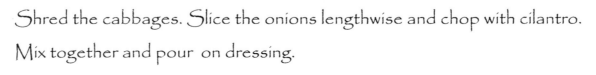

In Hawaii, many types of noodles are used.
Some are used in saimin with a good broth. Others are seasoned with vegetables and a little oil, stir-fried in a wok, for Chow Fun. The somen noodle is a white, thin noodle that takes only 2 minutes to cook.
There is a salad prepared here that is very refreshing!

Somen salad is a simple salad made by creating a bed of greens with Romaine or Bibb lettuce; (preferably a very green lettuce). The noodles are prepared, never overcooked, and given a cool rinse in a colander. Lift them apart to cool faster.
An oriental dressing is made with vegetable oil, sesame oil, sugar, rice vinegar, and some light miso paste.
The cooled noodles are placed on top of the bed of greens, and the dressing is poured on. She might add sesame seeds.
Garnish with chopped green onions and cucumbers.
Sometimes she just uses papaya seed dressing.
It is sweet and wonderful.

Her first Somen Salad was given to her as a gift from a girl who she met in her first week on Maui. She never forgot that!

Lomi Lomi Salmon

Amaryllis prepared her first lomi lomi salmon for a Christmas Day in Hawaii. She surprised all her local friends and family! To prepare the lomi salmon she started the day before. She sprinkles fresh raw salmon with Hawaiian salt (the rock-like natural sea salt) and lomi-lomis (massages) it in. She lets this soak over night on a bed of ice. When ready, she drains the water, minces the salmon and adds lots of minced tomatoes (Romas, or cherry tomatoes, or any ripe ones). She also minces Kula onions, the sweet kind, grown on the cool slopes of Haleakala. If it is too salty, she adds more ice and a little water. It is the perfect salty balance with poi.

2 lbs salmon filets
4 Maui sweet onions
8-10 Roma tomatoes
Hawaiian salt

Massage the salt into the salmon, set on a bed of ice and refrigerate overnite. Drain the water. Mince the salmon, onions, tomatoes and combine. If it is too salty add ice.

serve with Poi

Kahlua Pork

She also prepared a pork loin in an attempt to create kahlua pork. She seasoned the pork with Hawaiian salt and placed it on a rack in a roasting pan . Water was added beneath the rack, with liquid smoke to create a smoky flavor. She smothered the top of the pork loin with guava jelly to give some sweetness, and covered the whole thing in foil to seal in the juices, but left a little tent-like formation to allow some venting of the steam. She cooked this large pork loin for 2 hours at 325 degrees. The meat was shredded and served on a platter with the lomi salmon, poi, grilled apple bananas and grilled pineapple slices.

6-7 lb Pork butt or Pork loin
Hawaiian sea salt rubbed on all sides
Liquid smoke, 2 oz. into the water below the pork
Guava or passion fruit jelly on top for sweetness!
Roast in the oven at 325 degrees, or covered grill on low heat
    for two hours until the meat will pull apart easily.

Enjoy the smoky flavor!

The water is the secret to the moisture!

Babies love poi, and it is highly nutritious.

To mix a 1 lb. bag of Poi, add 3/4 ~1 cup of water gradually while squeezing and mashing poi still in the bag. Continue squeezing and mashing until blended. Then pour into a bowl. Twist bag to get every last drop. Taste & enjoy!

Amaryllis keeps it at room temperature with a plate over the bowl or refrigerates it with a layer of water on top to keep it from drying out.

Poi

Amaryllis first experienced Poi at a breakfast served by local friends in Waikiki, with scrambled eggs and toast and found it unappealing. Little did she know that many years later she would acquire a taste for it, and love the essence of the root of the taro plant.

Poi is made from the bulbous root of the Taro plant. The "corms" are washed and cleaned of all the rooty filaments, and dropped into boiling water. When tender, they are mashed, and water is added to the mashed taro root to a consistency like a pudding.

There are many varieties of Taro.
Each has its own unique flavor. Amaryllis loves the flavor of the root. Depending on the type of taro, and the location where it is grown, it takes on a different flavor.

There is a difference in fresh water grown taro, and dry land-grown taro root. She loves Keanae poi, Hana poi, Hanalei Kauai poi, and especially loves 3-day poi, when it has a slightly sour taste.

Once, she had not yet boiled her taro, and experienced a rash on her arms. She had met others who were sensitive to the white juices in certain taro leaf stems.

She loves poi best when complemented with lomi-lomi salmon. Her mother-in-law likes a little sugar added.

Hawaiians planted taro to avoid starvation, and they planted with a passion.

They filled the valleys from the mountain to the sea. They used all the parts of the plant. The taro leaf or luau leaf is used to wrap fish or pork and adds amazing flavor. These are called lau-lau.

Lau Lau

Put 4-5 taro leaves, with stems removed in the hand and place pieces of pork, chicken, beef and butterfish on top with a little Hawaiian salt on chicken and beef. Put 3 more luau leaf on top. Place lau lau on the end of a ti-leaf with rib removed and wrap up tightly.
Wrap with another ti-leaf and tie with string or rib of ti leaf. The lau laus are steamed.
40-60 lau lau take 4-6 hours in the steamer.
They can be done in a pressure cooker for 1 and 1/2 hours at 15 pounds pressure.

Lau-Lau is sometimes prepared with the luau leaf and then wrapped in foil, without the ti-leaf outer wrapping. This is wonderful too.

Some insist it needs the ti-leaf to be the best!

Baked Taro

The root is scraped on all the outside, washed & cleaned and baked the same as potatoes for about one to one and a half hours, then salted and buttered.

Luau Leaf

Young Taro leaves are put into hot water and, when they have boiled 10-15 minutes, the water is poured off through a colander, then more water is poured into the pot, with milk or coconut milk, over the leaves and boiled until the leaves lose their form and are very tender. It is seasoned with salt and pepper. The milk helps lose the "sting" which some luau leaf has. Amaryllis had read the old Hawaiian cookbooks, and consulted with her sister in law, before preparing her first luau leaves.

She knew she loved luau leaf flavor, and she craved it so she had to know how to prepare it.

The first time she ever saw squid luau was at a big birthday luau in Hana. She thought the appearance of the dark green cooked leaves wasn't pretty, but the flavor was incredible.

This particular preparation was sweetened with coconut milk and was so delicious.

When the lau lau are made, the taro leaf is cooked inside the individual packages, when all the ti-leaf-wrapped bundles are placed in the steamer to be cooked.

Her brother-in-law said "some taro is more bitter, some the stems are so good, the others not."

Chicken Luau

4-lb. chicken
1 tbsp. salt
4 lbs. Taro leaves
3 cups coconut milk

Cut chicken into small
pieces. Put into large pot,
add salt and cover with
water.
Simmer until tender.
Wash luau leaves carefully.
Remove stems.
Place in a saucepan,
add 1 cup water,
cover and cook 15 minutes.
Drain.
Add water & repeat
process 2 more times.

Add coconut milk.

Serve chicken on platter
with a cup of the broth.

Add Luau sauce.

Ono!

Tahitian Taro

was best for the coconut style.

The Chinese huge leaves were what she tried first.
Her honey arrived home with huge leaves and stalks in his hand
like a giant bouquet. The leaves are 2 feet in length. Wow!

She tore the leaves, and cooked them separately from the meat,
as instructed.

She drained them after 15 minutes, then after adding the new
water and cooking the leaves again for 10 minutes, she added
the cooked meat, which she had prepared with salt and pepper,
and garlic powder and minced onion flakes and covered in water
to cook for a couple hours.

She used a chuck roast, which she seasoned with salt & pepper
and browned first, then covered with water and turned it a few
times as the water level went down.

She then re-seasoned the taro leaf with a little salt and pepper
and butter and combined with the cooked meat.

It's absolutely delicious, and really easy, too.

Haupia

6 cans unsweetened coconut milk
1 cup sugar
1 cup cornstarch
1/2 tsp. salt

Mix all ingredients together
Heat until it comes to a boil.
Whisk cornstarch to dissolve,
then simmer until it thickens.
Pour into shallow pans and chill.
Cut into squares to serve.

Serves 12 people

Breadfruit

The "Ulu", or breadfruit, grows on a lovely tall tree with beautiful, broad, shapely leaves. The fruit is oval to round, and larger than a grapefruit. The meat is white. The skin has an inter-locking pattern on the surface with small circles within each puzzle piece.

When ripe, they are brown in color. The antique cookbook said: "If you like it sweet, wait 'til it is soft. Bake for one hour."

Amaryllis loves the addition of coconut milk when the breadfruit is nearly cooked (after peeling and cutting into small chunks, boiling in just enough water to keep from burning).

She first experienced breadfruit prepared by an old Japanese man for her girlfriends. He cut the breadfruit in half and then placed the halves face down on a baking sheet with some water underneath to steam it for about an hour.

Butter and brown sugar was added and it was delicious and satisfying.

Brown rice

2 cups water

1 cup rice

or 3/4 cup rice & 1/4 cup whole wheat berries that have been soaked for a few hours in hot water poured over them.

Put rice in the pot with salted water, and bring to a rolling boil, then reduce heat to a simmer and cover with lid. Simmer for 30 minutes, or until all the water is absorbed then turn off heat and leave the lid on until ready to serve.

White Rice

2 cups water

1 cup rice

Bring the rice and salted water to a boil then turn down to low and cover with lid, about 15 minutes, until all the water is absorbed.

If the rice has been rinsed, then less water will be needed because it has absorbed some of that water.

It was said to Amaryllis once, that a day without rice was a day without sunshine.

The Beauty of Simple Foods

There is such a beauty to simple foods, like whole-wheat (unprocessed) berries, and other grains like oats, millet and every variety of rice. Brown rice, wild rice, basmati rice, and white rice are a joy when cooked to perfection. Calrose is our favorite here in Hawaii for sticky rice needed for sushi. It plumps up so nicely and holds moisture. Jasmine rice has such a wonderful aroma, and so does basmati and pecan rice. There is something so soothing about the smell of rice cooking, or whole oats simmering. The simplicity and routine of washing and rinsing the rice to look for and remove any dirt or stones is pleasing to the soul.

She washes it until the water is clear.

An old man in Hawaii taught her how to make rice. First he taught her how to wash the rice several times and then drain it leaving the rice in the pot. Then he added water up to the first line of the index finger, for one cup rice, when the finger was touching the bottom of the pot. For two cups of washed rice, he brought the water line up to the second line of the index finger in a 1-qt. saucepan. Then the rice was brought to a rolling boil, turned down to a simmer and the lid placed on top. This was cooked until the water was absorbed (about 15 minutes). The heat was turned off and the rice could sit until ready to serve.

In Hawaii we all have rice cookers. These awesome cookers take the guesswork out of rice cooking. They vary in price from twelve dollars to over one hundred dollars for the more elaborate, airtight, Japanese rice cookers. To be accurate with washed rice, she uses one and one half cups water to 1 cup rice.

Teriyaki Sauce

3 cups soy sauce
1 cup water
1 cup granulated sugar
10 ~20 cloves garlic smashed
1/4 cup fresh grated ginger root, unpeeled
1/2 cup honey

Teriyaki Chicken

Cover the chicken in the soy teriyaki mixture to marinate at least two hours in the refrigerator. Remove chicken to a clean baking dish, with some of the marinade poured over. Bake at 350 degrees for 1 hour.

You may cook in the frying pan with 2 tbsp. vegetable oil to brown the meat then cover with some of the teriyaki marinade and cook about 45 minutes ~ 1 hour.

Grilling is the best way to cook teriyaki.

On the grill

Follow the rules about chicken.
Wash hands frequently!
Don't baste with the marinade.
Discard the uncooked sauce.

Enjoy the Beauty!

Teriyaki Chicken

She could make teriyaki chicken in a heartbeat. She prepared the marinade to soak the chicken for at least a few hours or overnight. She learned from two girls who owned a restaurant in Lahaina, Maui. They had a recipe for a teriyaki tofu pita. Sliced tofu was baked in the teriyaki blend of ginger, soy sauce, garlic, sugar and water. After they baked the tofu, they drained the large slices, then placed them into a pita sandwich, with a variety of sprouts (alfalfa, mung bean, sunflower), a homemade hummus, and a delicious tahini (sesame) dressing. They taught her to start with lots of soy sauce (3 cups), plus 1 cup of water. The girls mashed whole heads of garlic, which were placed inside Ziplocs and pounded with a mallet, or the side of a large knife handle, until all the skins came off and the essence of garlic was released.

A cup of sugar and 1/4 c. fresh ginger was added, which she always stores in her freezer. She tastes the mixture for sweetness and saltiness, and adds water or sugar. She puts drummettes on the grill for 30-45 minutes depending on the size. Everyone on the beach can take in the delightful aromas. She grills pineapple, red and yellow peppers, onions, tomatoes, zucchini, and eggplant, buttered and seasoned with garlic, Parmesan, brushed with olive oil and an herb brush. (Fresh herbs tied to the end of a wooden spoon; these impart wonderful flavors to the grilled foods). In a heartbeat, once she was awakened by her honey, who said: "We're going to Makena"! the most beautiful beach on Maui. She jumped out of bed, pulled ice-glazed chicken out of the freezer, rinsed it, poured off the water, and put it in a bag with soy sauce, water, pre-minced garlic, ginger & sugar. She shook the bag and placed it in an ice chest to marinate.

The most memorable events can happen spontaneously like that.

Enjoy the moment!

Be ready!

Love Life!

carry a grill in the car

(make sure the fire is completely out!)

Sometimes she adds honey to make Teriyaki chicken sweeter and more easily browned. The fragrant ginger completes the marinade. She lets it soak, turning now and then to coat evenly. When it is cooking, in the oven or on the grill, it smells so delicious.

She is reminded of the beaches along the coast of Kihei, Maui. As she passes by the Kamaole Beach Parks, she loves how the smell of teriyaki beef and chicken is in the air!

Sometimes she would take her grill right down to the beach and make her own fire. At a special beach where this is possible, she would dig a hole in the sand, down to where the sand is hard, and place rocks along the sidewalls to hold her grill and the sand in place.

She collects Kiawe wood to burn. (It's the best for flavor, also called mesquite). She starts with newspaper and twigs to build the fire, and never uses flammable liquids. When the coals are ready, she grills her teriyaki and the wonderful garlic and ginger aromas can be taken in by everyone on the beach!

Amaryllis thinks, "wow, this is living!"

Sushi

In Hawaii, Amaryllis learned to make the popular maki sushi. Her mother-in-law showed her how to prepare the sushi rice with 1/2 cup sweetened rice wine vinegar added to 4-6 cups cooked Calrose rice when it has cooled. She adds slowly and decides if it is the right texture. They sauteed a can of tuna in oil with 2 tbsp. vegetable oil sweetened with 1 tbsp. sugar and 1 tbsp. rice vinegar until it carmelized. They scrambled 4 eggs, cooked them in a pan, with a tbsp. of oil, like a flat pancake. They sliced the cooked eggs into thin strips & set aside. She layed out nori (dried seaweed sheets) on her bamboo sushi rolling mat and pressed rice onto the layer leaving the edges free. Tuna mixture is sprinkled along the length along with the egg strips. She could add thin sliced cucumber or carrots at this time and daikon sprouts. She proceeds to roll it up tightly by turning it over once inside the mat then rolling the mat to the end to close the roll. It takes practice but it is not hard to make beautiful maki sushi. Make sure the rice is not too wet! The nori must retain some crispness to be excellent! Seal the end with a moistened finger. She likes to make special hand rolls with crab, avocado, shrimp, cucumber, daikon sprouts, asparagus, and spicy mayonnaise. She prepares steamed rice (no vinegar). She spreads the cooled rice across the nori, then layers crab, shrimp, avocado, daikon sprouts, cucumber strips, steamed and cooled asparagus, and spicy mayonnaise (two tbsp. mayo with 1 tsp sesame-chili oil, & 1 tsp. red pepper sauce). She wraps in a cone shape overflowing with goodies. Dip in wasabe shoyu.   Buy a bamboo rolling mat.

4-6 cups cooked rice	nori sheets	scrambled egg	mayonnaise
rice wine vinegar	vegetable oil	sugar	cucumber
daikon sprouts	sesame chili oil	tuna	red chili sauce
asparagus	crab & avocado	carrots	cooked shrimp

Portuguese Bean Soup

The Portuguese all make their bean soup slightly different! Amaryllis does hers two different ways. One is a quick style and the other is a slow cook. The quick style requires canned kidney beans, and the slow cook uses dried kidney beans which have been soaked overnite. For quick style she uses a hamhock and a Portuguese sausage for flavor, with onions, garlic, salt and allspice. She browns the meat, add the onions, garlic and spices, then covers with water to simmer. She adds 2 chopped carrots, 2 cans kidney beans with the juice, and 16 oz. tomato sauce. This simmers into a rich soup within one hour. Ready to serve

1 Portuguese Sausage
1 onion, minced   1 clove garlic
2 cans kidney beans
1 hamhock
salt and pepper
1/2 tsp. allspice
2 carrots chopped
16 Oz. tomato sauce

Slow Cooked Portuguese Bean Soup simmers for 2 hours on low. She seasons a pork butt with salt and pepper, browns it and adds the minced onion and spices. She covers with water & simmers with the beans for about an hour then adds the carrots and tomato sauce. She continues to simmer for a total of two hours, and at the last 10 minutes she adds a big bunch of chopped kale or watercress.

1 Pork Butt, salt and peppered and cut into small pieces
16 oz.-bag kidney beans soaked overnite.
1 bunch kale or watercress

Seared Sea Scallops

12 large sea scallops
2 tbsp. olive oil
1 shallot, minced
2 cloves garlic, minced
2 tbsp. butter
1/2 cup white wine
fresh herbs

Heat olive oil in a pan on medium high.
   Add the garlic and shallot, then the scallops.
      Sear the scallops on high, then lower heat.
      Add the butter to blend the flavors.
   Serve the scallops over rice.

Add fresh thyme or tarragon and Chardonnay wine
to deglaze the pan. Add cream to make a rich sauce.

Garnish with fresh limes and long pieces of chives!

Serve with salad & rice!

She Loves Shrimp

Amaryllis prepares her shrimp in a big pot of water with herbs, salt and olive oil. When the water boils, she drops the peeled shrimp gently in small amounts (about 1 pound at a time) and cooks just until they are pink. (About 1-2 minutes). Shrimp must never be overcooked or they'll be tough, not succulent and awesomely delicious. She quickly drains and gives a quick cool rinse or plunges them into ice to stop the cooking, and serves on a platter with fresh sliced lemons and limes and three dipping sauces (A cocktail sauce, a Thai sweet chili sauce, and a Louis sauce). Sometimes she does Scampi, using butter and olive oil with lots of minced garlic. The olive oil keeps the butter from burning, while the butter gives the wonderful flavor. She butterflies all the shrimp first. She buys fresh or frozen raw tail on de-veined type shrimp, which makes them easy to prepare. Rinse frozen shrimp in a colander to thaw. To butterfly, one must run the knife down the center back, cutting nearly half way through the shrimp without cutting it apart. (This filets them open and makes them seem twice their size). She adds the shrimp and when they have turned pink, she adds a splash of Chardonnay to poach for a minute with some fresh herbs like a sprig of thyme or rosemary. The Scampi is served on a bed of rice with a bright vegetable, like snow peas or crisp green beans, or on pasta with all the juices from the scampi tossed to coat the noodles or bows or spaghetti. She adds Parmesan or Romano cheese and lemon zest for added zing! She uses medium to large shrimp that are so plump and decadently satisfying! She serves 10-15 shrimp on each plate! It's a wonderful dinner for two, followed by an awesome dessert like crème brulee with a passion fruit or raspberry sauce or a decadent chocolate mousse!

Ingredients for Coconut Panko Shrimp

2 lbs. shrimp (tail-on deveined)
panko flakes (rough or fine)
1 bag sweetened coconut flakes
4 eggs
vegetable oil

Butterfly all the shrimp and lay on platter.
Lightly beat eggs in a bowl.

Put panko flakes in another bowl.
Put grated coconut on another plate or mix with panko flakes.
Dip shrimp in egg mixture then into panko/coconut mixture
and set aside. You can double dip in egg-panko-egg-coconut!
When all are coated heat 1/4 inch of oil in skillet.
Test the oil by placing one coated shrimp into the hot oil.
If it begins to bubble and cook, proceed to add several more.
Turn them as they get golden brown. Cook about 4 minutes,
then remove and drain on paper towels.   *Enjoy!*

Louis Sauce

1/2 cup mayonnaise
4 shakes Worcestershire
1/4 cup ketchup
lemon juice
1 clove fresh garlic, minced
horseradish, if you like!

Mix together & chill.

Buy Thai Sweet Chili Sauce in Asian section of market!

Coconut Panko Shrimp

There is Panko Shrimp, and there is Coconut Panko Shrimp, and they are delightful! Panko flakes are dried white breadcrumbs. Some are grated very finely, others are in large flakes and are more textured. Amaryllis butterflies large shrimp and lays them out on a platter. She has one bowl of beaten eggs, another of panko flakes, and another with the coconut; or the panko can be mixed with the shredded coconut. She dips the shrimp in the egg mixture then into the panko/coconut and sets aside until all are coated. Then she heats her vegetable oil and tests one shrimp to see if the oil is the right temperature. If it bubbles and begins to cook, it is ready. All the shrimp are added slowly, and turned as they get golden brown. Then they are drained on paper towels and served with dipping sauces, like soy with a tsp. of sesame oil, sugar, green onions, rice vinegar, and a little water, or Thai sweet chili sauce. Coconut Panko Shrimp is like a dessert in itself. It is crisp and flaky, succulent and sweet.

These are excellent pupu, in Hawaii, or appetizers anywhere in the world.

Shrimp Boil on the Beach

For a casual setting, like the beach, Amaryllis might do a shrimp boil, with shell-on type shrimp. Into a pot of boiling water she would add peppercorns, a bay leaf, oregano, chili peppers, cayenne, olive oil, salt, and the shrimp with shells for about 4 minutes until bright pink. She lifts out the shrimp with her strainer and serves them with fresh lemon wedges, melted butter and corn on the cob!

Appetizers

In Hawaii we called them pupu. We love to offer a variety of snacks to eat with beer, or just to share with our company. Amaryllis will tell you that it's easy to cook and prepare big parties, as you learn many dishes, that can be prepared in advance and combined for great effect!

She prepares her baked basil-mayonnaise salmon filets cut into 2-inch squares, as hot appetizers served beside chilled shrimp cocktails.

She prepares Swedish meatballs and teriyaki chicken drummettes before guests arrive. She loves Dim Sum, wonton skins wrapped around delicious morsels of pork, or chicken, with peas, or mung bean sprouts, minced onion, grated carrots, and oyster sauce, or hoisin sauce. All ingredients are available in the Asian sections of the market.

She forms and stuffs the little packages, folds them over and seals them with a flour-water mixture and her fingertips, then steams the stuffed wontons in a covered pot with a steamer, or in a bamboo steamer placed above a pot of steaming water. Sometimes she fries dim sum in oil for a crispy, tasty won ton.

Another nice appetizer she learned was a lomi salmon stuffed cherry tomato. Bite size treats!
She loves lox, too (Cold smoked salmon). She serves it on wheat or sesame crackers or triscuits, with wasabe cream cheese, bread and butter pickles and capers.

Swedish Meatballs

2 lb. lean ground beef
1/2 lb ground pork
1 small minced onion
4 eggs
1 cup milk
1 cup bread crumbs
fresh or dried thyme
salt & pepper

Soak breadcrumbs in the milk and add to the meat mixture.
Roll into small meatballs and brown in butter.
Remove from pan and create the gravy by adding two tbsp. flour
to the drippings, stirring vigorously. Then add 1 cup of milk,
heat until bubbling and the mixture thickens.
Add salt & pepper to taste
Put meatballs back into the gravy to finish cooking.
If too thick, add a little water and reheat.
Season as necessary.

Ground Turkey Meatballs

She does turkey meatballs with 1 pound ground turkey, 3
eggs, minced onions, 1 cup milk, Italian breadcrumbs, salt and
pepper, garlic powder, and thyme mixed together, rolled into
balls, and browned in olive oil, then set aside. She finishes
them with a gravy, or continues cooking them in a marinara
sauce to serve with pasta. They are lower in fat, and have
plenty of flavor. Try it! (You could teriyaki them also.)

Dim Sum

   Wonderful little packages are filled with ground pork hash, delicate morsels of fresh peas, bean sprouts and sauce then steamed in bamboo baskets over hot water. The Chinese make homemade dough for these stuffed won tons. You can buy them as won ton skins in the markets.

Cooked ground crab, chicken, pork or pork sausages
small minced onion
minced carrot, few tbsp.
minced celery, few tbsp.
fresh or frozen peas
mung bean sprouts
hoisin sauce (plum sauce)
oyster sauce

Mix together cooked meat, onions, carrots and celery.
Place a tbsp. on won ton wrapper.
Place a few peas & bean sprouts on top.
Add a few drops of either sauce.
Fold in half and seal edges with flour paste or an egg wash.

Steam in bamboo steamer or any kind of steamer, or deep fry in oil and drain on paper towels.

Dipping Sauce

1/2 cup soy sauce
2 tbsp. sesame oil
1/2 cup water
chopped green onions
1 tbsp. sugar

Potato-Macaroni Salad

Amaryllis Style

10-12 medium potatoes
1 lb. bag of macaroni
2 cups chopped celery
1/2 cup grated carrots
1 cup minced onions
3/4 cup bread-&-butter pickles, minced
10 hard-boiled eggs
salt & pepper
2 tbsp. Dijon mustard
1 cup mayonnaise

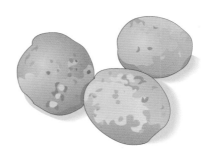

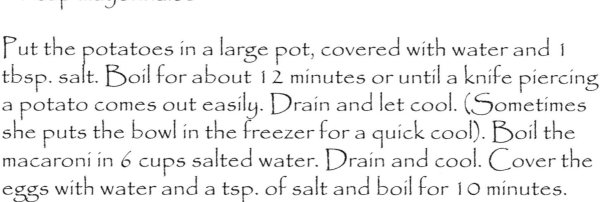

Put the potatoes in a large pot, covered with water and 1 tbsp. salt. Boil for about 12 minutes or until a knife piercing a potato comes out easily. Drain and let cool. (Sometimes she puts the bowl in the freezer for a quick cool). Boil the macaroni in 6 cups salted water. Drain and cool. Cover the eggs with water and a tsp. of salt and boil for 10 minutes. Cool under cold water.
Peel and chop for potato - mac salad.

Combine cooled chopped potatoes and macaroni together.
Add celery, onion, pickles, boiled eggs, salt and pepper.
Add the mayonnaise and mustard. Taste and season!
This is always awesome.
Make sure you have just the right amount of mayonnaise.
    (Not too much, not too little.)
She always adds more pickle juice, salt and pepper.

Famous Cheesecake with Graham Cracker Crust

3 packages cream cheese, softened
4 eggs
1 tsp. vanilla
1 cup sugar

Blend with electric mixer.
Crush 2 pkg. graham crackers (she uses bottom of measuring cup to crush).
Pour 1 stick melted butter over and mix together.
Press into pie dish or bottom of spring form pan.
Pour cream cheese mixture into pie shell and bake at 350
   degrees for 45-50 minutes until firm.
Remove & cool while preparing sour cream topping.
Beat 8 ounces sour cream with 2 tbsp. sugar, 1 tsp. vanilla and
spread over cheese cake.
Bake for 5 more minutes at 200 degrees, with oven cracked
open slightly. Keep plain or when cool, add favorite fruit topping and chill.
Slice and serve with fresh brewed coffee or tea, to everyone's delight!

Desserts To Delight

Everyone should know how to prepare some excellent desserts by heart. Amaryllis has her favorites. Try new things and add them to your repertoire. During the holidays, she prepares all her best. She prepares beautiful pies and perfect piecrusts. She learned the perfect piecrust recipe from a lady on the Big Island of Hawaii. Amaryllis has elaborated on the perfect piecrust as she learned more in gourmet magazines. Always receptive to new ideas, cooking for her is the most exciting art! Her Black-Russian cake wins everyone at Christmas! Her Pineapple-Carrot cake, with luscious cream cheese frosting, has so much texture, with nuts, raisins and pineapple in a bundt-cake style. She bakes her famous cheesecake with a sour cream topping and graham cracker crust, and varies the topping from cherries, to blueberries, strawberries or just plain. Her apple pie with crumb topping is great year-round.
Crème Brulee is now her favorite!

Black Russian Cake

1 yellow cake mix
4 eggs
1 cup vegetable oil
1 small instant-chocolate pudding mix
1/4 cup vodka
1/4 cup kahlua
3/4 cup warm water

Beat together on high 4 minutes, bake in an oiled, lightly floured bundt pan at 350 degrees for 45-60 minutes, until toothpick comes out clean. Make a glaze of powdered sugar, a little cocoa powder, kahlua and vodka beaten together and drizzle over bundt cake! Try adding an instant pudding mix to any cake recipe for incredible moistness.

Apple Pie with Crumb Topping

She chooses tart green apples such as Granny Smith or pippins, and sometimes mixes two kinds for an interesting twist. She mixed Fuji apples with tart apples recently, for a wonderful pie. She peels, cores and slices 7-9 apples in large pieces. She squeezes lemon juice over them to keep their color. The apples are combined with 1/2 cup sugar, 2 tbsp flour, 1 tsp cinnamon, 1/4 tsp cloves, 1/4 tsp allspice, and sometimes cardamon, and tossed together to coat. Some use cornstarch or tapioca as a thickener, instead of flour, to keep it clearer. She prepares the perfect piecrust in advance. It is kept in a Ziploc bag in the refrigerator to chill for an hour.

Perfect Piecrust

2 c. flour   1 stick cold butter plus 1/3 cup Crisco
6-10 tbsp. ice water   1 egg yolk
2 tbsp. sugar   pinch of salt

Cut chilled butter and Crisco into the flour, sugar, and salt. Add the yolk, and ice water, and work into a nice consistency. Add flour, if too wet, butter or a little water, if too dry. Roll into ball. Chill in ziploc bag for 1 hour. Egg yolk gives a golden color and the sugar browns it nicely!
This recipe is for a two-crust pie so two pies can be made if using the crumb topping. It becomes so enjoyable to create any pie. It's so easy and satisfying. Divide the dough in half and roll out the crust. Flour a wooden board or table and flour the rolling pin often. Roll out the dough to the size of your pie. It should be about ¼-inch thick. Loosen it from the board or table with a spatula slid all the way around on all sides. Lift the dough and place it into the pie plate and press it into place. Amaryllis makes a few slits on the bottom crust.

The apple mixture is piled into the pie plate and topped with the crumb topping.

Crumb Topping

1/3 cup flour
3/4 cup light brown sugar   (recipe is for one pie)
1/3 cup butter

She mixes flour and sugar to a consistency of coarse sand, cuts in the butter to make a crumbly mixture. She piles it on the pie & bakes at 400 degrees for 15 minutes then lowers to 375 for 40 minutes, until bubbly. She makes a collar of aluminum foil 2 inches wide in 2 long pieces attached around the pie to avoid burning the edges of her crust! She loves fresh fruit pies made with whatever is in season.

In California, when driving the back desert roads, she came upon peach farms and brought home flats of fragrant peaches. She baked beautiful two-crust pies piled high with peaches. Anytime fruit is baked in a crust, it is sweetened, a thickener is added with cinnamon and spices, and dotted with butter for flavor. Moisten the edges with water or an egg wash to seal between the two crusts, shape into a pleasing design, decorate tops with leaves, star shapes, moons, and flower petals, moistened with flour & water to attach. She pierces the top to vent for steam and brushes with egg yolk or cream and sprinkles sugar to make them a golden brown. She adds liquors for exciting flavor and juiciness. She added rum to a pumpkin pie last year, creating a unique flavor.

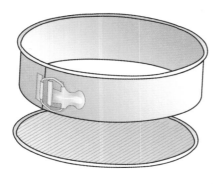
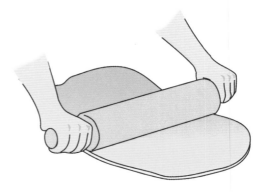

Baking pies brings happiness!

Sweet Potatoe Pie

is very similar to pumpkin pie. The yams are baked in the oven at 400 degrees until done. The skin is removed and they are cooled, then mixed with evaporated or whole milk, eggs, sugar, cinnamon, allspice, cloves, nutmeg, ginger and vanilla and poured into an unbaked pie shell and baked at 375 degrees for 55-60 minutes, until it puffs up and is firm to the touch in the middle. They puff up beautifully and hold their shape very well!

Prepare the perfect pie crust recipe for two pies.

Bake 4-5 yams in the oven at 400 degrees for 1 hour. Remove the skins and set yams aside to cool.

In a large bowl, mix:
3 eggs
2 cups of cooked yams
1 cup brown sugar
1/2 cup granulated white sugar
2 tbsp. molasses
1 & 2/3 cups evaporated milk
2 tsp. vanilla
1 tsp. cinnamon
1/4 tsp. nutmeg
1/2 tsp. cloves

Blend the mixture and pour into two unbaked 9-inch pie shells or 1 deep dish pie shell, and bake at 375 degrees for 1 hour or until firm to touch in the middle.

Scones

2 &1/2 cups all-purpose flour
1/3 cup sugar
1 tbsp. baking powder
1 & 1/2 sticks butter cut
        into 1-inch cubes & chilled
3/4 cup heavy cream
1/3 cup dried fruit
        or fresh berries

Preheat oven to 375 degrees
Combine flour, sugar and baking powder. Mix in a large bowl.
Add the butter and mix on low. Stir in fruits.
Make a well in the center and pour in cream.
Mix gently just until combined. Place scoops of batter one
inch apart on baking sheet. Brush scone tops with cream.
Bake for 12-16 minutes until scones are golden.

Try blueberries, dried cherries, rasberries, cranberries, chocolate,
raisins, currants, dried apricots, dates, mango, papaya, whatever!

Beautiful Breakfasts

include fresh fruits, juices, whole grain cereals, breads, like scones, muffins, coffee cakes, pancakes, waffles, French toast, pastries, and of course, perfect eggs and side dishes of sausage, bacon, or ham. To make perfect eggs, she insists you must know how long to cook them and various methods of preparing them. When people say they can't boil an egg, she says nonsense! To boil eggs, she puts enough water to cover the eggs and 1 tsp. salt. She brings it to a boil, then turns it down to medium for ten minutes. She immediately drains off the hot water, fills the pot with cold water to cool them and make them peel easily. (She loves egg salad on toast. Mash 2 hard-boiled eggs with a fork, blend with a tbsp. mayonnaise). Poach eggs with a tsp. vinegar added to the water to keep their shape. Try a hollandaise sauce!

French toast is made with 4 eggs, 1/4 cup milk, 1 tsp. vanilla and 1 tsp. cinnamon stirred together, then slices of bread are soaked in eggs, browned in a tbsp. of oil and served with butter, syrup and sprinkled with powdered sugar.

For *perfect scrambled eggs*, she turns the bowl while whisking them to fluffiness. There should not be any white unwhisked. She heats 2 tbsp. of butter on medium until it separates. She adds the eggs and, as they cook, moves them with a spatula. She folds them for about three minutes. Cheese is added just before they are finished. She loves them moist and hot. Cheese is grated, crumbled, sliced, or torn and distributed. Sometimes she adds fresh spinach cooked in the same pan a little to the side, and *feta, Swiss cheese, & Parmesan* just before serving. Whole grain or sour dough toast, marmalade, guava or passion fruit jelly, fresh squeezed orange juice with a fresh strawberry, and delicious coffee or tea makes a beautiful breakfast complete!

melettes are another story. She remembers years ago, a restaurant in Waikiki called Toulouse Lautrecs. It was an outdoor café with a rustic elegance. There were white linen tablecloths and fresh flowers. They served perfect omelettes in many varieties. There was even a cream cheese & jelly omelette. The bread was whole grained and her favorite omelette was the

Spinach Swiss Cheese Omelette.

You'll know it when you discover what you love, and must have it again and again.

2 tbsp. butter
6 large eggs
a handful of fresh spinach leaves
1/2 cup feta cheese, crumbled
Swiss cheese sliced
Parmesan, powdered
or grated
salt and pepper

To make a perfect omelette she starts with fluffy whisked eggs, usually 4-6 for two people. She has all her ingredients prepared in advance on the side, like grated cheese, spinach leaves, Parmesan, salt and pepper. She heats her non-stick pan with a tbsp. of butter on medium heat and, when the butter begins to separate, she pours in the eggs. It is critical that the heat is not too high, because an omelette should never be browned. She lets the omelette cook, on medium heat, without touching it for a few minutes, and she has a little trick she learned. To get the top cooked before she flips the whole thing, she takes a few drops of water and slowly drips them along the edge; (a little trick she learned for perfect omelettes).

Suddenly, the omelette begins to puff up and ruffle in the pan, as the water bubbles and begins to steam the topside of the omelette. She lowers the heat and covers for a few moments to steam, then prepares to flip her eggs. She slips the spatula under the whole thing and loosens it from the bottom and, with confidence she flips it over to finish off the other side. Immediately, she fills the top with her spinach leaves topped with Swiss cheese and Parmesan and folds the omelette in half. Then she sprinkles on more Parmesan or grated cheese and removes it from the heat, covers with a lid to let the cheeses melt and flavors blend. Sometimes a slice of tomato that has a chance to simmer on the bottom is wonderful. A touch of tarragon in scrambled eggs is really nice. Eggs should be fluffy, moist and always served hot.

They are not appealing if served cold.

It takes practice, but is so rewarding and fun when you get it down to how you like it. (Perfect!)

Basic Sauces

A basic white sauce is a Béchamel. Two tbsp. of butter are melted, then 2 tbsp. of flour are added and stirred vigorously to remove lumps, incorporate smoothly and cook off the flour taste. A cup of milk is added to make a sauce, stirring all the while and heating it to a nice creamy mixture. Salt and pepper are added. Variations are then created by adding bouillon to create rich flavor or cheese to create a Mornay!

Sweet tasting juices of canned peaches or pears (in heavy syrup) can be added to 2 tbsp. butter and 2 tbsp. powdered sugar to create a wonderful sauce for crepes or pancakes. She makes sauces from citrus juices, and peanut butter thinned to desired consistency while heating to enhance the flavors of added garlic, green or red chiles, and 2 tbsp. of oil for Thai satay dipping sauce.

Gravy is intimidating to some, but not to Amaryllis.

Once she was invited to a Thanksgiving Day party and knew no one there. It was so last-minute, that she had nothing prepared. The hostess prepared the huge turkey in her little apartment sized stove. All the guests arrived with various dishes. Amaryllis offered to make the gravy. That was her contribution to the party.

The bird was moved to the side and she began by heating up the wonderful drippings, just like her mother taught her. She placed the roasting pan over both front and back burners on the stove. She stirred to loosen any crispy turkey or stuffing pieces in the pan, and got it all bubbling. She added 2 tbsp. of flour and stirred vigorously with her wooden spoon. On the side she had stirred 1 tbsp. of flour into a glass of warm water. When all the lumps were dissolved she added the flour water to the paste and, suddenly there's gravy.

She maintains the heat and cooks to the desired consistency. Salt and pepper and a touch of broth are added if there were not enough drippings. The flour taste is cooked off within a few minutes and the flavor develops into rich gravy. On Thanksgiving, a turkey without gravy is like something's missing! (Until she tried Vingadoyzh)...

Vinha De Alhos

On Maui, when Amaryllis met her Portuguese boyfriend she was introduced to the world of Portuguese cooking. His father loved to cook Vinha De Alhos! (pronounced vinga doyzh.) The vinha is the vinegar brine used to soak the meat or fish before they're roasted. Four days before Thanksgiving, Richard takes a cleaned, thawed bird and places it in the roasting pan. He pours ½ gallon of apple cider vinegar over it and adds spices like garlic powder, onion flakes, allspice and a few cups of water. He places it inside a large plastic bag. It goes back into the refrigerator to marinate in the vinegar bath. He turns it several times over the next three days to distribute the brine. Somehow, by osmosis, the turkey takes in the juices and flavor. He drains off all the vinegar and returns it to the pan. Under the skin of the bird he stuffs pieces of butter. The skin is rubbed with vegetable oil, sprinkled with salt, covered with foil and baked at 350 degrees for the first half hour, then lowered to 325 degrees, as instructed (20 minutes per pound). The foil is removed the last hour to brown the skin. Pierce the skin and the juices just flow! They fill the pan with wonderful juice like never before. The turkey is removed to the side to cool and all the meat is removed by shredding or pulling it off the bones. The dark and light meats are combined together onto a large platter.

The juices are reheated to pour over the turkey!

Ingredients for Vinha De Alhos

1/2 gallon apple cider vinegar
used for turkey, chicken, pork, or fish
1 part water
3 parts vinegar
onion powder, salt and pepper
allspice
garlic flakes
1 bay leaf
peppercorns

Rinse meat and dry with paper towels, then add the brine, soak overnight up to 3 days for turkey; turn each day, and baste in the fridge. Drain off the liquid, place in the roasting pan, salt inside and outside of the bird. Stuff butter under the skin of the breasts and rub with oil, then put into pre-heated 350 degree oven for first half-hour. Lower heat to 325 degrees and cook as instructed, 20 minutes per pound. Remove foil for the last hour, so the bird can brown. Richard prepares his dressing outside of the bird. (It would get too wet inside this type of preparation.) The family can't wait to taste the Vinha De Alhos (vingadoyzh). People seem to love their own parents' style at the holidays, because that is what made their memories so rich. Amaryllis likes to please all, so she prepares two turkeys now. She prepares a turkey the night before, in the Vingadoyzh style, and, on Thanksgiving Day, another, stuffed with her favorite style of bread stuffing with sage, apples, walnuts, raisins, celery, onions, and sausage. She does a whole-cranberry sauce using the fresh juice of an orange that is bright and delicious. Her family loves the canned, jellied kind but this new version was so well received.

Boil together 1 cup of sugar, 1 cup of water, the juice of 1 orange, and 1 bag of cranberries til they pop!

Stuffings

Amaryllis loves to make stuffings for turkeys, chickens, pork roasts, even a large butternut (acorn) squash, and small pumpkins! She starts with toasted bread cut into cubes, sauteed celery and onions, browned sausage, and adds tart apples, raisins, butter, broth for moisture, chopped sage or other herbs for flavor and freshness from the garden! She adds chopped walnuts or slivered almonds. The stuffing is mixed in a bowl by hand. She packs it loosely into the bird or squash.

The flavors blend and taste delicious.
    She takes it out of the bird immediately!
        She cuts the pumpkin open in quarters like a flower
            to serve on a platter.
                Stuffings are wonderful!

Ingredients for stuffings

3 cups cubed bread or cooked rice
1/2 lb. cooked sausage
celery, onions, grated carrots, sauteed
1 cup nuts and 3/4 cup raisins
   or other dried fruits
1 apple chopped fine
1 cup vegetable or poultry broth for moisture
butter for flavor
spices like sage, thyme, rosemary, curry
Always remove stuffing from the bird immediately!

Try a crab stuffing for big shrimp or peppers, with bread crumbs, minced celery, green onions, mayo, lime juice, and cilantro! Blend ingredients, stuff, then bake!

Yeast Breads & Quick Breads

Amaryllis thinks everyone should try breadmaking to feel the wonderful joys of kneading the dough, watching it rise, smelling the fresh-baked, home-made goodness and happiness that comes with slowing down to enjoy breadmaking! It just feels so good! Many will say they don't have time, so she suggests learning just one recipe, like dinner rolls, for a special occasion to get inspired and to see how easy it is to bake yeast breads. You will be amazed!

Parker House Rolls: (she uses a basic recipe from Joy of Cooking)

1 package active dry yeast
   dissolved in 2 tbsp. hot water
1 cup warm milk
1 egg

3/4 tsp. salt
2 & 2/3 cups flour
pinch of sugar
       sifted into bowl.
1 tbsp. sugar

1 tbsp. sugar is dissolved in milk, a lightly beaten egg is added and then combined with the flour and yeast mixture. Knead it on a floured board only enough to form a nice soft dough (not sticky). She covers it with a dish towel and lets rise to double in size. She punches it down to let rise again. Then she forms small balls, places into muffin tins (three balls to each to make clover rolls, or several balls to one large pie pan to make break away rolls.) They rise again and are baked at 400 degrees for 15 minutes or until golden brown.
Awesome hot fluffy rolls!

Baking bread is good for the body, mind, soul, and spirit!

Awesome Banana Bread is so easy!

She starts with seven ripe bananas mashed into a bowl. She sifts flour, baking soda, cinnamon and salt into a bowl. She creams together butter and sugar, adds a 1/4 cup of honey and a tsp. of vanilla to the butter mixture, then adds the lightly beaten eggs. She combines the wet and dry ingredients and adds a cup of chopped walnuts, a cup of raisins stirred in at the end, and pours the batter into 2 oiled loaf pans, or several mini loaf pans to bake at 350 degrees 45-60 minutes until done! Sometimes she adds yogurt or 1/2 cup sour cream to the mixture. Many quick breads, like pumpkin bread and zucchini bread, are done this way. It's so easy!

7 ripe mashed bananas
2 & 1/2 cups flour
2 tsp. baking soda
1 tsp. salt
1 tsp. cinnamon
2 sticks butter at room temperature
1 & 1/2 cups sugar
1/4 cup honey
4 eggs, lightly beaten
1 tsp. vanilla
1 cup crushed walnuts
1 cup raisins

Pumpkin Bread is so moist and wonderful!

Cream cheese is delightful on this bread.

3 cups all-purpose flour
1 tsp. cinnamon
1 tsp. cloves
1 tsp. nutmeg
1 tsp. baking soda
1/2 tsp. salt
1/2 tsp. baking powder

1 cup vegetable oil
1 cup brown sugar
3/4 cup white sugar
3 large eggs
16 oz. can pumpkin pie filling
1 tsp. vanilla
1 cup chopped nuts (if you like)

Sift the flour, spices, baking soda, salt and baking powder into a large bowl. Beat the oil and sugar in another bowl and add the eggs and pumpkin and vanilla. Combine wet and dry ingredients. Add the nuts. Pour into 2 oiled and lightly floured loaf pans or nonstick type loaf pans.

Bake in 350 degree oven for 1 hour and 10 minutes (until toothpick or bamboo skewer comes out clean.)

Cool loaves on wire rack and enjoy!

Mango Bread is a Hawaiian favorite.

In May, throughout all the islands the mangos are ripening!
It's time to eat them like crazy, and preserve them if possible.
Quick breads can be frozen to enjoy at a later date.

2 cups flour
2 tsp. baking soda
2 tsp. cinnamon
1-1/2 cups sugar
1 cup shredded coconut
2 cups chopped mango
3/4 cup vegetable oil
3 eggs beaten
2 tsp. vanilla

Sift the flour, cinnamon and baking soda into a bowl.
Stir in the mango, coconut and oil, sugar, eggs and vanilla.
Bake in preheated oven at 350 degrees 1 hour and 15 minutes, or until done.

As you can see, quick bread recipes are all baked at 350 degrees for about an hour or until done. Temperature and length of cooking time vary from sea level to the higher mountain elevations!

Chicken can be done a hundred different ways. Amaryllis prepares a whole chicken by cleaning it, rinsing and patting it dry, and salting the inside, just like her turkey. She always rubs it with vegetable oil so it will brown nicely. Amaryllis loves crisp skin that has so much flavor. She rubs salt, pepper and spices and drizzles oil over that. She stuffs the bird, or cooks it with vegetables inside, like chopped carrots, celery, and onions, adds butter and fresh thyme. She loves to pick fresh herbs. It is so satisfying to step into your garden and pick your harvest! A chicken is cooked 1 hour and 15 minutes.

Tandoori chicken is Indian-style curried chicken baked in a clay oven. Amaryllis prepares a marinade of ginger-garlic paste, lemon juice, chili powder, plain yogurt, garam masala powder, salt and 2 tbsp. vegetable oil and refrigerates chicken pieces in this marinade for two-three hours. Then she puts small chicken pieces on wet bamboo skewers to bake in the oven at 350 degrees for 15-20 minutes.

Chicken drummettes are prepared teriyaki style with a ginger, garlic, sugar, water, soy sauce and honey marinade then cooked in a pan, a dutch oven or baked in the oven or on the grill. *Buffalo wings* have a tomato-ketchup sauce base with chili powder, pepper flakes, cayenne, vegetable oil, honey, mustard, ginger-garlic, chili sauce and Worsestershire sauce.

Katsu chicken filets are dusted with flour, dipped in egg & panko flakes! They are cooked in oil like panko shrimp! *Papaya chicken* is baked. A sauce of citrus juices, soy sauce, brown sugar and corn starch is boiled with sliced papaya, cooked 10 minutes and poured over it.

Hawaiian Curry: Saute onions and apples in 2 tbsp oil. Add 2 tbsp. butter, 2 tbsp. flour, 1 tbsp. curry powder, then 1 can coconut milk and chicken broth. Heat with ginger and garlic. Cooked chicken or crab is added 'til hot!

Chicken & Dumplings requires the basic chicken soup. Then a dumpling mixture is prepared with 2 cups flour, 1 tbsp baking powder, 1 tsp salt, 4 tbsp shortening, 2 eggs lightly beaten, 1 cup buttermilk or milk, and finely chopped parsley. The mixture is combined just until mixed so it remains fluffy. Spoonfuls of the dumpling mix are dropped into the broth and poached for 15 minutes. Add salt and pepper!

Lemon Chicken is one of Amaryllis' favorites. She slices two lemons and layers them with sliced yellow onions among chicken pieces with the skin on. She puts butter on top of the chicken breasts, sprinkles them with garlic salt and pepper. She drizzles on a tablespoon of vegetable oil to make the skin crisp but flavored with the butter. She bakes at 375 degrees 15 minutes then lowers to 350 dgrees for 45 more minutes. The lemon is so refreshing and bright!

BBQ chicken is good cooked in the oven or on the grill. She makes a sauce from a cup of ketchup, 3/4 cup of brown sugar, a few shakes of Worcestershire, the juice of one lemon, crushed fresh garlic cloves, 2 tbsp molasses, 2 tbsp honey, a tbsp mustard, and minced onion. She drizzles vegetable oil over chicken pieces, adds salt and pepper and places in a preheated oven at 375 degrees for 15 minutes. She whisks the sauce, then pours it over the browned chicken, lowers the heat to 350 degrees for 45 more minutes or until done.

Chicken Parmesan is prepared with boneless skinless chicken pieces brushed with olive oil, garlic, and fresh herbs (rosemary, thyme and basil), browned in butter then baked in marinara topped with mozzarella & Parmesan cheese!

Fried Chicken is so ono! Marinate in a batter of buttermilk & spices (salt, pepper, oregano, cumin, cayenne). Dust with spiced flour. Fry in small batches.
Drain on paper towels!

Potatoes can be simply elegant!

They can be boiled, baked, scalloped, au gratin, roasted with herbs, mashed, seared in a little oil as a pancake, whipped and piped into puffs, or cut into shoestrings.

Amaryllis loves

Twice baked potatoes.
She washes big russets
and wraps them in foil
She bakes them at 400
degrees for 1 hour.

When they are done she opens the foil, slits the potatoes in half, and scoops out the potatoes into a bowl, carefully leaving the skin and foil intact. She mixes together butter, sour cream, minced green onions or chives, salt and pepper, and sometimes cooked filet mignon pieces.

She spoons the mixture back into the skins and grates cheddar cheese over the tops and bakes again for 20 minutes at 350 degrees until the cheese is melted and the potatoes are hot! They are so creamy and delicious!

Mashed potatoes are boiled until tender then whipped with butter, cream or half & half, salt and pepper! She makes garlic mashed potatoes that are excellent!

She would love the instrument that spiral cuts vegetables into slinky shoestrings for a totally flamboyant effect!

Let's Party

To prepare for parties, she imagines her menu a few days before and plans her shopping list. She has lots of pupus ready when guests arrive to keep them entertained and happy!

Favorite Amaryllis Party Foods

Shrimp coctail platter with three dipping sauces
Panko Coconut Shrimp
Dim Sum steamed or fried and soy sesame sauce
Teriyaki chicken drummettes or teriyaki beef
Baked Salmon Filets with basil & mayonnaise

Layered salad with spinach, mesclun mix, bibb lettuce, fresh herbs, feta, raisins, mandarins, and honey vinaigrette
Vegetable platters with Dill-ginger dip
Local style potato-macaroni salad, poi, lau lau, lomi salmon

A *whole fish* poached or baked and served with a bechamel.

Pork loin seasoned with a dry rub of spices, salt and pepper, seared in olive oil then baked at 300 degrees for 2 hours, or 1 hour then completed on the grill. (Juicy) Slice to serve.

Seasoned steaks with Worcestershire, salt, pepper, and garlic flakes, grilled medium rare, and cut into diagonal slices, or *shishkebobs* are always awesome! She loves lamb seared in olive oil with rosemary and a touch of lavender. Season with salt & pepper!

Party Desserts in Hawaii

Guava chiffon cake, chocolate dobash cake, haupia, lilikoi (passion fruit) chiffon pie, pineapple-carrot cake and creme brulee are all served in Hawaii.

Amaryllis makes a frozen mango dessert in a blender from fresh or frozen mango, ice cubes, fresh ginger, cinnamon, sugar or sugar substitute, and milk, soymilk, rice milk or 1/2 & 1/2 .

Mango Smoothies for two

3 large ripe Haden mangos peeled and sliced
    or 2 cups frozen mango
1 banana
4 ice cubes
2 tbsp fresh grated ginger
1 cup milk, soymilk, rice milk, or 1/2 & 1/2
1 tsp cinnamon
4 tbsp sugar or 3 packages splenda

In a blender, pulse on high to crush the ice and blend the fruit.
Add more milk if necessary to blend.
Serve in large goblets with a sprig of mint.

If you use less milk it will be a thicker frozen dessert!

Guava Crisp requires about 12 medium guavas sliced and dusted with 2 tbsp flour and 1/2 cup sugar, heated in a pan to bring out the flavors and juices. Layer in a baking dish and prepare the crumb topping and crumble on top. Bake at 375 degrees for 30 minutes until bubbly and crisp! It's a really nice dessert done with peaches, apples, mangos or any fruit. She learned this in Puna Hawaii on the Big Island where guavas are so plentiful!

Crumb topping: 1/3 cup flour, 3/4 light brown sugar, 1/3 cup softened butter. Mix the flour and sugar to a consistency of coarse sand, cut in the butter, then crumble on top of the fruit!

Guava Chiffon Pie: Dissolve 1 tbsp. plain gelatin in 1/4 cup of water. Add 1/4 cup of sugar, and 2/3 cup guava puree to 4 well beaten egg yolks. Cook on low heat until thick, stirring constantly. Remove from heat, blend in gelatin and cool. Add lemon juice and guava juice. When beginning to set, fold in 4 stiffly beaten egg whites to which 1/2 cup sugar and 1/4 tsp. salt has been added. Pour into pre-baked pie shell and chill.
Garnish with whipped cream!

1 tbsp. gelatin
1/4 cup water
3/4 cup sugar
2/3 cup guava puree
1/4 cup lemon juice
1/4 tsp. salt
4 eggs separated

pre-baked pie shells are baked for 15 minutes with something to weight them down like dried beans, rice, or ceramic weights on foil, then remove the weights and return to oven for 5 more minutes to finish.

Lilikoi Iced Tea:

Ten lilikoi are cut in half. The skin and pulp are covered with purified water in a sauce pan and boiled twenty minutes. The wonderful smell of lilikoi fills the house. Cool the mixture and strain over tall glasses filled with ice. Then add more water to dilute and add sweetener. It's the most delicious refreshing fragrant iced tea that takes her back to the old days in Hawaii when she first arrived on Maui!

Lilikoi Chiffon Pie:

Soften 1 tbsp plain gelatin in 1/2 cup cold water. Put 4 egg yolks, 1/2 cup sugar, a dash of salt and 1/3 cup lilikoi juice in double boiler. Mix well, and cook over double boiler until thick and foamy, stirring constantly with electric mixer; about 3 minutes. Remove from heat and add gelatin.

Mix well and cool. Beat 4 egg whites until stiff and add 1/4 cup sugar gradually. Then fold into gelatin mixture. Pile lightly into baked pie shell and chill until set. Makes a 9-inch pie.

1 tbsp. gelatin
1/2 cup cold water
3/4 cup sugar
1/3 cup lilikoi juice
dash salt
4 eggs, separated

try lemon chiffon pie with the same recipe

Use a metal bowl over a saucepan for the "double boiler".

Lilikoi Salad Dressing,

1/3 cup of oil, 1/4 cup lilikoi juice (strained), 2 tbsp. white vinegar, juice of 1 lemon, 2 tbsp sugar or honey are whisked together and served. Wonderful!

Creme Brulee

She always wanted to learn to make Creme Brulee. She attempted 2 different recipes from the Food Network, and decided she liked the one that required scalding 1 pint of heavy cream in a double-boiler; combining 5 eggs yolks with 5 tbsp. sugar, and vanilla, in a separate bowl, adding hot cream slowly to the egg mixture, then returning to the double-boiler and whisking until it thickens. It has to be tempered to avoid curdling the eggs so if the water is too hot underneath, remove bowl every so often while whisking and return to heat. When it thickens to a beautiful custard, pour into buttered souffle dishes and chill. Sprinkle on brown or turbinado sugar and place under broiler until sugar melts and carmelizes. Return to fridge until ready to serve!

Drizzle with a rasberry, lilikoi, or mango syrup.

1 pint heavy cream
1 tsp. vanilla
5 eggs yolks, beaten lightly
5 tbsp sugar
1 cup brown sugar

Scald the cream in a double-boiler
Whisk the egg yolks with granulated sugar.
Add hot cream slowly & return to double boiler.
Whisk until it thickens being careful not to overheat!
Pour into buttered souffle dishes and chill.
Sprinkle brown sugar thickly and broil until carmelized!
Chill again until ready to serve and drizzle with lilikoi syrup.

Garnish with spearmint!

Try adding cocoa or espresso powder to the mixture!

Guava Jelly & Other Preserves.

Amaryllis learned to make jams and jellies one day. She made 500 jars her first time. The "secret" was to follow directions explicitly for sugar and certo measurements, and to use fresh lemons to keep the color bright. Pamela told her "You must use a stainless steel pot and while heating the fruit to a rolling boil, you take a spoon and rub it along the side of the pot to see if it gels. Then you know it is ready to pour into jars." First, she prepared rasberry preserves. It was the most vibrant, ruby red color and had excellent flavor. One batch came out thinner and was used for ice cream topping! For strawberries, lemon kept the color beautiful and bright! She likes liquid Certo, but works without it, too! *Use equal amounts of fruit and sugar. Try any fruit!* For apricots, she picked the fruit off the tree laden with fruit. She blanched the fruit by placing it in boiling water for 1 minute, then in cold water to remove the skins; then returned it to the stainless steel pot to prepare the preserves. She even learned to make pectin by collecting the juices from blanched apples placed in a pillow case to drain over a bowl in the sink overnight. Mint jelly was created with pectin, mint extract, and a few drops of green food coloring. It is excellent with lamb dishes.

Guava Jelly

Use guavas not quite ripe. Remove blossom end. Cut into quarters, put into a stainless steel pot with water just enough that it shows between the fruit. Boil 'til the fruit is very soft. Strain the mixture. Measure exact amounts of fruit juice and sugar and bring to a boil for 15 minutes. When done, pour into sterilized glasses (which have been boiled in water and not removed until jelly is ready.) Seal with wax or use airtight lids. Try lilikoi jelly, too! Always add lemon juice.

Have fun and enjoy!

©Marilyn Jansen 2005

Molokai

Be happy!

Kauai

enjoy life!

Oahu

live aloha

live in the moment!

Maui

Hawaii

Lanai

Niihau